Contents

Dreams and legends

Everyone dreams of flying.
People have always wanted to be able
to fly. They looked at birds flying
overhead. What did birds have that
people did not?

Wings.

In Ancient Greece an inventor
called Daedalus made wings
of wax and feathers. He and
his son Icarus strapped the
wings to their arms and flew.
But Icarus went too high.
The hot sun melted the wax,
his wings came apart and
Icarus fell into
the sea.

This is only a legend, but for thousands of years people thought that if they made wings they would be able to fly like birds or bats.

Many died trying. They strapped on their wings and jumped off cliffs and high buildings. But still birds and bats could fly and humans could not.

Something was wrong.

The first men in the air

When people did get into the sky, it was not with wings.

In 1783 the first hot-air balloon was launched. This was a huge bag of air, with a basket of fire underneath.

But a balloon cannot be steered. It goes where the wind takes it. People still longed to fly like birds, going wherever they wanted.

Flying was not so easy as it looked.

Did you know...

Hot air is lighter than cold air. When the fire heats the air in the balloon, it goes upwards.

 **Heavie**

With a ball
were not rea
were ins

At last they saw where they were going wrong. Humans could never fly by strapping on wings and flapping them.

They would have to invent a flying machine and travel inside it.

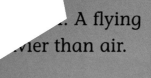
. A flying
...ier than air.

ground?

Did you know...

There were many ideas about what this flying machine might look like. Some were sensible and some were strange.

⬅ Gérard 1784

The flying machine

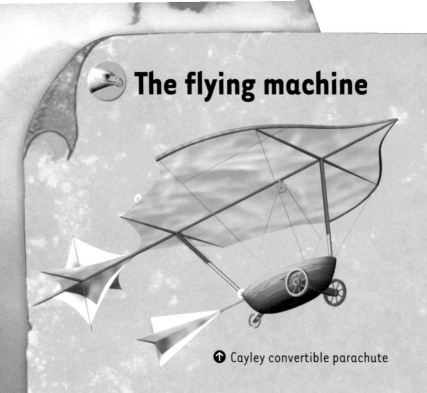

⬆ Cayley convertible parachute

An Englishman called George Caley designed a heavier-than-air machine that could glide, but it could not fly. Like a bird it had wings and a tail but there was one important difference. The wings were fixed, they did not flap.

Between the wings and the tail was a long body, called the fuselage. Most aeroplanes are built like this today.

Caley's machine still could not get in to the air. It needed an engine. But this was in 1799. The right kind of engine had not been invented yet.

It would be nearly one hundred years before a human being flew like a bird.

↑ Cayley triplane

↑ Cayley convertiplane

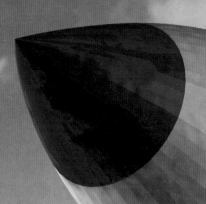

The race to fly

In the late 19th century airships were built in France. These were sausage-shaped hydrogen balloons with engines. They could be steered but they were still lighter than air.

A heavier-than-air machine had to have an engine to get it off the ground and wings to keep it up.

This machine had a name, **aeroplane**, but nobody had built one yet. Who would be the first?

The race to fly was on.

Santos Dumonts airship.

The bird man

The first man who really flew
was a German called
Otto Lilienthal.

Lilienthal built hang-gliders. He ran downhill to take off and made long gliding flights. He spent many hours watching birds flying and wrote a book about it.

Lilienthal died in a flying accident but people in America were already reading his book.

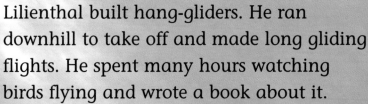

This is what Lilienthal noticed; a bird's wings are not flat and stiff. They have the same kinds of bones in them as we have in our arms and hands.

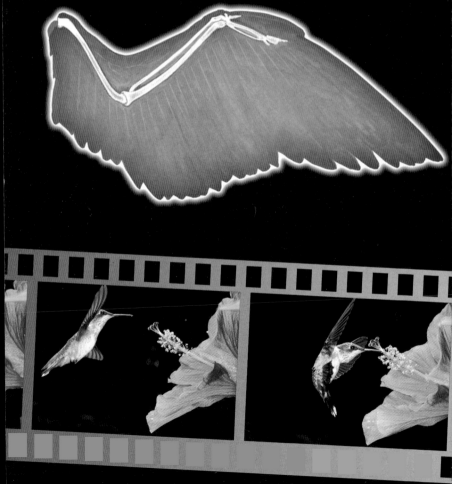

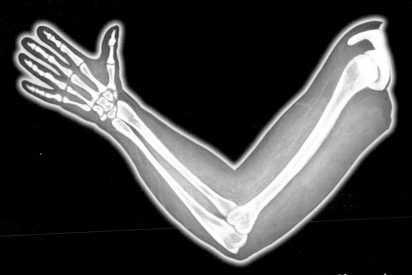

Human arms can move in many different directions. So can birds' wings. When a bird flies its wings change shape. The feathers in the wings and tail help it to gain height and to steer. The wings on an aeroplane must be able to change shape.

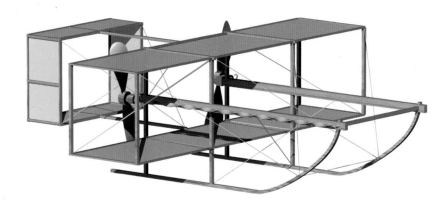

The Wright brothers

Wilbur and Orville Wright were
Americans who ran a bicycle business.
They were also inventors and engineers
and they planned to fly.

- They did not rush things.

- They read Lilienthal's book about bird flight.

- They studied all the other flying machines
  that could not fly.

- They did experiments with models and gliders.

- Then they built a machine with an engine.

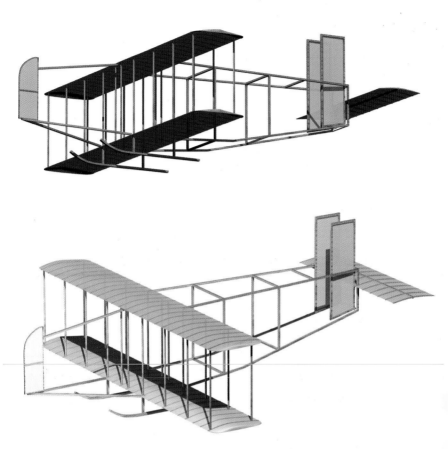

◆ ◆ These are the
Wright brothers' models.

It had a moveable tail to steer with,
and wings that could be warped – the
person in the machine pulled wires to
make them change shape like a bird's
wings. They called it *Flyer*.

One day at the end of 1903, Orville lay in *Flyer* and started the engine. *Flyer* rose in to the air under its own power and Orville, warping the wings, kept it airborne for 12 seconds.

He was the first person to fly in a
heavier-than-air machine.

How did Flyer fly?

It was not driven into the sky by the engine, like a rocket. When *Flyer* was going fast enough, the shape of the wings stopped the air pressing down on them. The air under the wings helped to lift the machine.

◗ Cross-section of wing showing airflow

aileron

The next new idea was the aileron.
This was a flap at the back of the wing
that could be moved up and down.
It had been designed in 1868 but there
was no way of using it then.

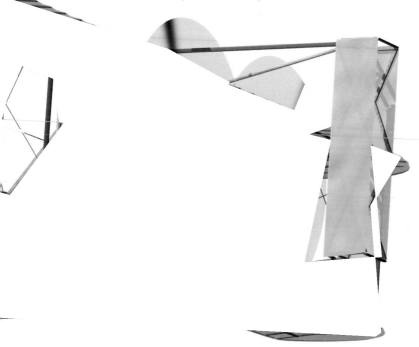

**No more pulling wires to warp the wings –
the aileron changed the shape.**

What is a plane?

Six years after Orville Wright
first flew, Louis Bleriot crossed
the Channel by air, from France
to England.

Bleriot's aircraft was a monoplane.
The Wright brothers' *Flyer* was a
biplane. Which part of an aeroplane
is the plane?

The plane is the wing. *Flyer* had
two wings, one above the other.
The pilot lay on
the fuselage in
the middle of
the bottom wing.

Bleriot's monoplane had one wing in two parts, one each side of the fuselage. Modern aeroplanes have one wing in two parts. These wings are so big that fuel tanks are built inside them.

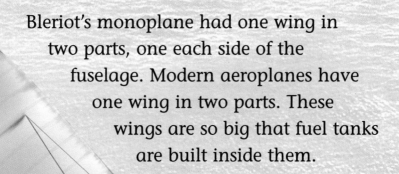

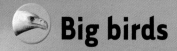# Big birds

These days some airliners can stay in the air for hours and travel thousands of miles, but they still work in the same way as *Flyer*. They have engines to get them off the ground and wings that change shape to keep them in the air.

When a great modern airliner comes in to land, machinery makes the wings increase in size so that it almost glides down.

So, after all, people were not so silly when they tried to fly like birds. But first they had to find out how birds fly.

Glossary

airliner
An airliner is an aircraft that
carries passengers.   **28**

bi-
This is part of a word. It means
having two of something.
A biplane has two wings.   **26**

designed
When something is designed, it
is planned and drawn before it is
made.   **30**

engineer
Engineers know how to make
machines and understand how
they work. They also design
buildings, bridges and tunnels.

20

hydrogen
Hydrogen is a very light gas.

14

increase

To increase means to get bigger.

28

inventor

An inventor thinks up new ideas. These do not always work.

6, 20

legend

A legend is a very old story. It may be about real people but it is not true.

6

mono-

This is part of a word. It means one or single. A monoplane has one single wing.

26

warp

To warp means to twist into a different shape.

25

Reading Together

Oxford Reds have been written by leading children's authors who have a passion for particular non-fiction subjects. So as well as up-to-date information, fascinating facts and stunning pictures, these books provide powerful writing which draws the reader into the text.

Oxford Reds are written in simple language, checked by educational advisors. There is plenty of repetition of words and phrases, and all technical words are explained. They are an ideal vehicle for helping your child develop a love of reading – by building fluency, confidence and enjoyment.

You can help your child by reading the first few pages out loud, then encourage him or her to continue alone. You could share the reading by taking turns to read a page or two. Or you could read the whole book aloud, so your child knows it well before tackling it alone.

Oxford Reds will help your child develop a love of reading and a lasting curiosity about the world we live in.

Sue Palmer
Writer and Literacy Consultant